The Story of Me

*Babies, Bodies,
and a Very Good God*

STAN & BRENNA JONES

A NavPress resource published in alliance
with Tyndale House Publishers, Inc.

NavPress is the publishing ministry of The Navigators, an international Christian organization and leader in personal spiritual development. NavPress is committed to helping people grow spiritually and enjoy lives of meaning and hope through personal and group resources that are biblically rooted, culturally relevant, and highly practical.

For more information, visit www.NavPress.com.

The Story of Me: Babies, Bodies, and a Very Good God

Copyright © 1995, 2007, 2019 by Stanton and Brenna Jones. All rights reserved.

A NavPress resource published in alliance with Tyndale House Publishers, Inc.

NAVPRESS is a registered trademark of NavPress, The Navigators, Colorado Springs, CO. The NAVPRESS logo is a trademark of NavPress, The Navigators. *TYNDALE* is a registered trademark of Tyndale House Publishers, Inc. Absence of ® in connection with marks of NavPress or other parties does not indicate an absence of registration of those marks.

The Team for the Third Edition:

Don Pape, Publisher
Caitlyn Carlson, Developmental Editor
Jennifer Ghionzoli, Designer
Joel Spector, Illustrator

Cover and interior illustrations of birds, bees, and vine copyright © mightyisland/Getty Images. All rights reserved.

Photograph of authors copyright © 2018 by Michael Hudson Photography. All rights reserved.

Scripture quotations are taken from *The Holy Bible*, English Standard Version® (ESV®), copyright © 2001 by Crossway, a publishing ministry of Good News Publishers. Used by permission. All rights reserved.

For information about special discounts for bulk purchases, please contact Tyndale House Publishers at csresponse@tyndale.com, or call 1-800-323-9400.

Cataloging-in-Publication Data is available.

ISBN 978-1-64158-133-2

Printed in China

25   24   23   22   21
6   5   4   3   2

TO LINDSAY, AARON, AND JACKSON

ACKNOWLEDGMENTS

WE OFFER HEARTFELT THANKS to the many parents who have shared their stories and perspectives, praise and disagreements about the content of the five-book God's Design for Sex series as we have spoken and taught about this subject around the country and around the world. Some of your stories have made it into the revised versions of these books!

We remain thankful for our friends mentioned in previous editions, with whom we shared the joys and travails of the journey of parenting our young children through to adulthood and with whom we shared enriching dialogue about the ideas in this book. Continuing thanks also to thirteen generations of graduate students in Stan's Human Sexuality summer course (1983-95), whose insightfulness, openness, and inquisitiveness so enriched our understanding of sexuality, and whose stories of how they learned (or mostly not) about sexuality in their families were an inspiration for these books. Revisions to the second-edition children's books were enriched by the professional reviews of Steve Gerali and Elaine Roberts; special thanks to Susan Martins Miller for her editorial expertise on that edition.

As we prepare the third edition of these books, there are many whose help we are grateful to acknowledge: We owe special thanks to Wheaton College for its support of the scholarship of its faculty, particularly in the form of a spring 2017 sabbatical. Stan was encouraged in 2011 by the opportunity and invitation by the editors of *Christianity Today* to share the essence of our approach in the pages of that important journal.[1] Emily Verseveldt served as an outstanding graduate research assistant 2014-15, gathering and updating a great deal of material for the *How and When* book; Emily, you are a model of organization and resourcefulness. Thanks also to Amy Smith, who has served as Stan's research assistant since 2017 and provided additional research and critical proofreading. Dr. Glynn Harrison, professor emeritus of psychiatry at University of Bristol, gave us the enormous gift of his review of and suggestions for the entire five-book series, for which he has our everlasting gratitude.

We are pleased to welcome Dr. Mark and Lori Yarhouse as current reviewers and future collaborators on this book series. Stan had the honor of contributing to Mark's training in clinical psychology at the master's and doctoral levels at Wheaton College, and together they have coauthored a number of articles and books. Since leaving Wheaton, Mark has established a distinguished career as perhaps the most prominent Christian psychological researcher in human sexuality in the world. Lori has invested her energies with Mark in parenting and homeschooling their three children. Our intent is that they will progressively become more involved with future revisions of the series. No one deserves deeper thanks than the Yarhouses for their extraordinarily helpful review of the entire five-book God's Design for Sex series in both the second and third revisions.

Special thanks to our NavPress editor, Caitlyn Carlson, and the publisher of NavPress, Don Pape, for your wisdom, friendship, and tremendous support. We are grateful as well for the partnership between NavPress and Tyndale House Publishers.

Finally, we want to express our deep love, appreciation, and pride for our three (now adult) children. Thank you for being our initial living laboratory for working out these ideas, for the shape and texture of your lives today, and for being so thoughtful, strong, and loving. Thank you for the wonderful spouses you brought into our family, whom we love as our own children, and for our dear grandchildren. You have, together and individually, enriched our lives far beyond what we ever could have imagined.

PARENTS, GOD GAVE YOU your sexuality as a precious gift. And you're reading this book because God has given you a child you love as a gift flowing from your sexuality.

God gave your child the gift of sexuality as well. If handled responsibly, this gift will be a source of blessing and delight. How can parents help make this happen?

Many forces will push children to make bad choices about sex based on false beliefs and values and on misplaced spiritual priorities. These forces are more powerful, confusing, persuasive, and ever present today than ever in history, thanks to the power of social media and the confusion of our culture. From their earliest years, children are bombarded with destructive, misleading messages—messages about the nature of sexual intimacy, about marriage, about family, about the boundaries of godly sexual expression, and even about the basic creational design of humanity as male and female.

These messages come from everywhere—through music, television, the Internet, discussions with their friends, school sex-education programs, and many other sources. The result? Confusion, doubt, and shame, as well as distressing rates of sexual experimentation, teen pregnancy, abortion, sexually transmitted disease, divorce, and devastated lives.

We believe that *God means for Christian parents to be their children's primary sex educators*. First messages are the most powerful—why wait until your child hears distorted views and then try to correct the misunderstanding? Sexuality is a beautiful gift—why not present it to your child the way God intended? God's Word is trustworthy and true—why not teach your child how to understand and live by its guidance in the area of sexuality? Why not establish yourself as the trusted expert to whom your child can turn to hear God's truth about sexuality?

The God's Design for Sex series is designed to help parents shape their children's character, particularly in the area of sexuality. Sex education in the family is less about giving biological information and more about *shaping your child's moral character*. The earlier you start helping your child see himself or herself as God does, including in the area of sexuality, the stronger your child will be as they enter the turbulent teenage years.

How and When to Tell Your Kids about Sex is a parents' resource manual in which we offer a comprehensive understanding of what parents can do to shape their children's sexual character. The four children's books in this series are designed for parents and children to work through together. Those books are structured to be read with your child at ages three to five (*The Story of Me*), five to eight (*Before I Was Born*), eight to twelve (*What's the Big Deal?*), and twelve to sixteen (*Facing the Facts*). These age ranges are not strict formulas; you need to exercise your judgment about your child's maturity level, environment, needs, and so forth to decide when and how to introduce the books.

The four children's books are meant to provide the foundational information kids need. Further, they are to be starting points for you to build upon and personalize as you discuss sexuality with your child in an age-appropriate manner. They provide an anchor point for discussions in order to jump-start deeper explorations. These books help break the silence and put the issues out on the table.

Don't simply hand these books to your child to read, *because our whole point is to empower you as the parent to shape your child's sexual character.* The books are meant to start and shape conversations between you and your child and to deepen your impact on your child in the area of sexuality.

In this series, we address controversial topics about which Christians disagree, including masturbation, how far people should go sexually when they're dating, contraception, gender identity, homosexuality, and more. Our goal in doing so is not to presumptuously present our answers as completely right but rather to encourage you to reach reasoned conclusions and to teach your child as you see fit before the Lord.

We have tried in each book to present information that we believe children of that age must have, without presenting controversial topics "too early." Your child may be confronted with complicated and confusing issues at a much earlier age than you expect. In such cases, you can draw on our discussions in later books to inform your dialogue with your child. For instance, we hold off on discussion of sexual orientation until the book for eight-to-twelve-year-olds (*What's the Big Deal?*), and on discussion of gender identity and transgender issues until the book for twelve-to-sixteen-year-olds (*Facing the Facts*). But your child may need more basic information much earlier, and in such cases, we urge you to use or adapt material from this book and our books for older children to meet your child's needs.

Why start early? Because if you as the parent are not teaching your child about sexuality, your child will learn distorted lessons about sexuality from television, the Internet, and playground conversations. If you are silent on sex while the rest of the world is abuzz about it, your child will learn that you cannot help in this key area. If you teach godly, truthful, tactful, and appropriate lessons about sexuality, your child will trust you more and see you as a parent who tells the truth.

We'll briefly unpack each of the books at more length to help you discern which would be most helpful to you in your current parenting season.

PARENT RESOURCE: *How and When to Tell Your Kids about Sex:* A Lifelong *Approach to Shaping Your Child's Sexual Character*

This book is the parents' comprehensive resource manual for the God's Design for Sex series. We take on the hardest subjects, such as sexual abuse, gender identity, and homosexuality, helping you know when and how to bring up these subjects. Our goals for *How and When to Tell Your Kids about Sex* are to

· **HELP** you understand your role in shaping your child's character, including his or her views, attitudes, and beliefs about sexuality;

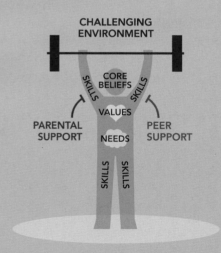

· **INSTRUCT** you in the twelve key principles for Christian sex education in the home and how to implement the strategies and tactics suggested by these principles;

· **FAMILIARIZE** you with the challenges that your child will face from secular culture and empower you with strategies and skills to help them overcome those challenges;

· **GROUND** your understanding of God's view of our sexuality;

· **EQUIP** you and your child to explain and defend the traditional Christian view of sexual morality in these modern times;

· **EXAMINE** each major developmental stage of your child's life and share age-appropriate information and approaches;

· **ADDRESS** directly the most complex issues you and your child might or will face in today's culture in a manner grounded in biblical thinking and informed by the best contemporary science;

· **EXPLORE** how you can most powerfully influence your child to live a life of sexual chastity; and

· **EQUIP** you to provide your child with the strengths necessary to stand by their commitment to traditional Christian morality.

As you read the following descriptions of each of the books for your child, please know that the concepts and issues presented in each of these books flow directly from the background provided by this foundational parents' guide.

Ages Three to Five
The Story of Me: Babies, Bodies, and a Very Good God

Your most important task with your young child is to lay a spiritual foundation for their understanding of sexuality. God loves the human body (and the whole human person), and the body is included in what God called "very good" (Genesis 1:31). Children's bodies, their existence as boys or girls, and also their sexual organs are gifts from God.

Young children can begin to develop a wondrous appreciation for God's marvelous gift of sexuality by understanding some of the basics of fetal development. In this book, we discuss the growth of a child inside a mother's body and the birth process. With such instruction, young children begin to develop a trust for God's law and to see God as a lawgiver who has the best interests of his people at heart. God is the giver of good gifts!

Finally, we want children to see families grounded on the lifelong marital union of one man and one woman as God's intended framework for the nurture and love of children. If you are reading the book as a single parent or with an adopted child, you will have opportunity to talk about how God sometimes creates and blesses alternative forms of families. We hope that you will find *The Story of Me* a wonderful starting point for discussing sexuality with your young child.

Ages Five to Eight
Before I Was Born: God Knew My Name
by Carolyn Nystrom, with Stan and Brenna Jones

Before I Was Born emphasizes the creational goodness of our bodies, our existence as men and women, and our sexual organs. This book introduces new topics as well, including the growth and changes boys and girls experience as they become men and women.

It includes a tactful but direct explanation of sexual intercourse between husbands and wives. God wants sexual intercourse limited to marriage, because sexual intercourse brings husbands and wives close together in a way that honors God and helps to build strong families.

Parents often ask, "Do my kids really need to know about sexual intercourse this early?" Remembering that you are the decision maker as to whether you use this book with a very mature five-year-old or with a more slowly maturing eight-year-old, the answer is yes. We believe this is a strategic decision parents must face based on their individual children, considering that first messages are always the most powerful messages. If, as a Christian parent, you want to begin to shape a godly attitude in your child about sex, why would you wait until they first soak in the misperceptions of the world? Why not build godly attitudes and views from the foundation up?

If you're reading this with an adopted child, use this opportunity to explain that not every couple will have biological children. If a baby doesn't grow in the wife's womb, the couple might look for a baby to adopt. And some women are not able to take care of a baby, so another family might adopt the baby and make it part of their family forever. Even though the baby grew inside a different mother, the husband and wife love this baby very much. Adoption is another way that God makes families.

Ages Eight to Twelve
What's the Big Deal?: *Why God Cares about Sex*

This book reinforces the messages of our first two children's books, covering the basics of sexual intercourse and the fundamental creational goodness of our sexuality. It continues the task of deliberately building children's understanding of why God intends sexual intercourse to be reserved for marriage.

This book goes further than the earlier books, adding more of the facts your child will need to know as they approach puberty. Further, it will help you begin the process of inoculating your child against the negative moral messages of the world. In *How and When to Tell Your Kids about Sex*, we argue that Christian parents should *not* try to completely shelter their children from the destructive moral messages of the world. If they mature in environments where they are not exposed to germs, children grow up with depleted immune systems that are ineffectual for resisting disease. When parents shelter their children too much, children are left naive and vulnerable; parents risk communicating that the negative messages of the world are so powerful that Christians cannot even talk about them.

But neither should you let your child be inundated with society's destructive messages. The principle of inoculation suggests that you should deliberately expose your child to the contrary moral messages they will hear from the world. It should be in your *home* that your child first learns that many people in our world do not believe in reserving sex for marriage, and it should be in your home that your child first understands such problems as pornography, teenage pregnancy, gay marriage, sexual identity and gender issues, and so forth. In this way, you can help build your child's defenses against departing from God's ways.

Facing the Facts: The Truth about Sex and You

Facing the Facts: The Truth about Sex and You builds upon all that has come before but also—in more depth—prepares your child for puberty. At this age, your child is old enough for more detailed information about the changes their body is about to go through and about the adult body they will soon receive as a gift from God.

In this book, your child will hear again about God's view of sexuality and about his loving and beautiful intentions for how this gift should be used. The distorted ways in which our world views sex must be clearly labeled, and your child must be prepared to face views and beliefs contrary to those they learn at home. We attempt to do all this while also talking about the many confusing feelings of puberty and early adolescence.

While children could read this book independently, we do not believe this would be optimal. We encourage you to read it alongside your child and then talk about it together. You could go chapter by chapter. Alternatively, you can read it and use it as a resource for important conversations with your soon-to-be or young teenager.

In this book, we address the most controversial topics of the series, topics about which biblically grounded Christians can and do frequently disagree. We make suggestions about appropriate moral positions on all of the important issues, including sexual-intimacy limits before marriage, masturbation, contraception, gender identity, homosexuality, and more.

We have joked that in each of these books, we are guaranteed to say something to lead almost any Christian parent to declare us too conservative or too liberal on some topic or to disagree with us somewhere. We do not presume our answers are completely right. At the very least, we hope our thoughts empower you, the parent, to think the matter through and present a better answer to your child as the Lord guides your thinking.

All of these books were written as if dialogue is an ongoing reality between mother, father, and child. Yet in some homes, only one parent is willing to talk about sex. Many Christian parents shoulder the responsibility of parenting alone due to separation, divorce, or death. Grandparents sometimes must raise their grandkids. We've tried to be sensitive to adoptive families and families that do not fit the mold of the traditional nuclear family, but we cannot anticipate or respond to all the unique needs of families. Use these books with creativity and discernment to meet the needs of your situation.

We hope these books will be valuable tools in raising a new generation of faithful Christian young people. If you follow this plan, we believe your child will have a healthy, positive, accepting, godly attitude about sexuality. As an unmarried person, your child will be more likely to live a confident, chaste life as a faithful witness to the work of Christ in their heart. If your child does marry, we believe they will have a greater chance of having a fulfilled, loving, rewarding life as a husband or wife. It is our prayer that this curriculum will encourage and equip you to dive into the wonderful work of shaping your child's sexual character.

ABOUT THE AUTHORS

STAN (STANTON L.) JONES, PHD, is a clinical psychologist. He recently returned to serving as professor of psychology at Wheaton College after serving for twenty years as its provost (chief academic officer). Earlier, he led in establishing Wheaton's PsyD program in clinical psychology. He has been a visiting scholar at the University of Cambridge and has published many articles in journals such as *American Psychologist*, *General Psychologist*, *First Things*, and *Christianity Today*. Beyond the God's Design for Sex series, his books include *Psychology: A Student's Guide*, *Modern Psychotherapies: A Comprehensive Christian Appraisal* (2nd ed., with Richard E. Butman), *Ex-Gays?: A Longitudinal Study of Religiously Mediated Change in Sexual Orientation* (with Mark A. Yarhouse), and *Homosexuality: The Use of Scientific Research in the Church's Moral Debate* (with Mark A. Yarhouse).

BRENNA JONES serves in a professional ministry of discipleship and support as well as spiritual counsel and prayer for women. She served as a leader in a Bible-study ministry with women for a number of years. She has graduate training in biblical and theological studies.

BRENNA & STAN wrote the original versions of their books on sex education while their three children were young; now they enjoy their three kids as adults, along with their kids' spouses and children.

"Tell me my story again, Daddy!"

"Okay. You're Paul Jackson, Sarah is your baby sister, you're four and a half, and you live in—"

"No, no! I don't mean that! I mean tell me where I came from! Tell me the story about *me*!"

"Oh, *that* story! We would be glad to! Mommy, would you start?"

"Sure!"

"Long ago, God knew all about our mommies and daddies, and their mommies and daddies. He knew about your father and me, and your sister and you. And he already loved us all! One reason God made Daddy and me is so we would love each other. Then we could have you and Sarah and love you both."

"And was that why I was born?
So that you would have a little boy to love?"

"Yes, and so that you could grow to love God with your whole heart for all your life. God also has some important work for you to do. When you live like Jesus and obey God's rules like Jesus, your life will help other people know more about God. And maybe you will get married and be a father yourself someday."

"And how did God make me, Daddy?
First, he started by having you and Mommy
love each other, right?"

"That's right! God made people so a man and a woman could love
each other, get married, and start a new family. Having a baby
is hard work because a little boy or little girl needs a lot of love.
When a mommy and daddy are married, they can both give their
child their own special kind of love, just what that baby needs."

*"Sometimes a mother knows she will not be able to give her baby
everything it needs. For example, a woman who has no husband
to help her and is very poor might let another mommy and daddy
adopt her baby so they can love and care for the baby."*

"Was I in Mommy's tummy right away when you got married?"

"No, God waited a few years. Then he took a tiny piece of Daddy's body and a tiny piece of Mommy's body, and made *you*! That is why you look a little like me and a little like Mommy. Even so, God does this in a way that makes you different from anyone else."

"At first you were too tiny to live out in this world. God put you inside my body in my womb. God made this special place so you could grow your heart and brain, arms and legs, eyes and fingers and toes. You grew until you were big and strong enough to hug and feed and play with! It takes about nine months to grow that big."

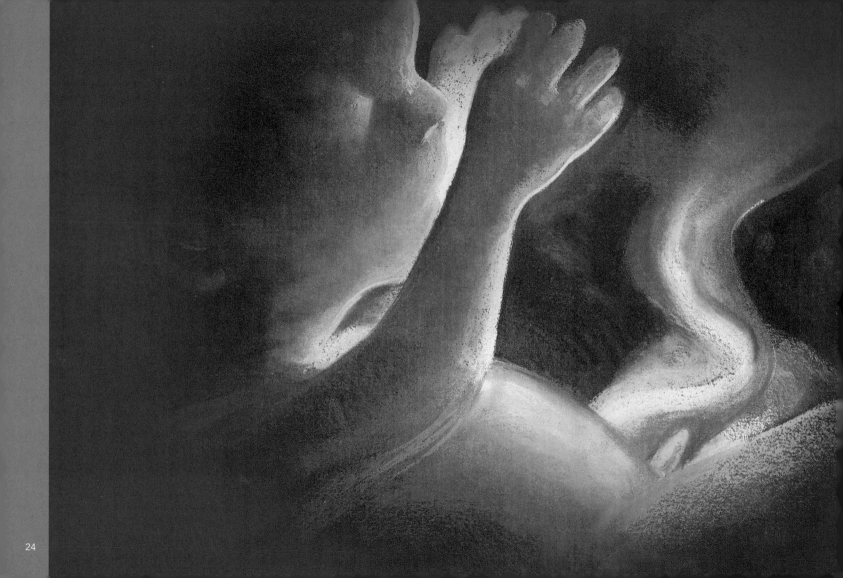

"But how could I breathe inside of Mommy or get anything to eat?"

"Good questions, Paul! God gives each baby an umbilical cord. It is like a hose from the mommy to the baby. Food and water and air go right through it from the mommy to the baby."

"Mommy, is that why I have a belly button?"

"That's right! When a baby is born, it doesn't need the cord anymore. The doctor cuts the umbilical cord. Your belly button is where your cord connected from inside me to you."

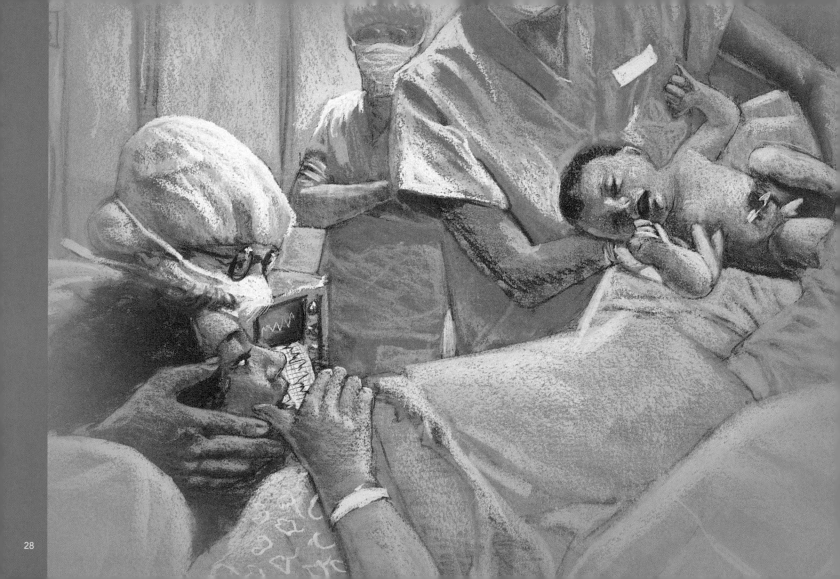

"Did your tummy get as big with me
as it did with Sarah? That big?"

"It did! And when the time was right, you came out into the
world through my vagina, which is part of my private parts.
I pushed really hard. God made my vagina so that it could
stretch just big enough to let you out. Daddy got to watch you
being born. It was like a miracle for him to see you come from
inside my body!"

"But Sarah didn't come out that way,
did she, Daddy?"

"No, Sarah was upside down in Mommy's womb. The doctor
decided to operate to open Mommy's belly and take Sarah out
of Mommy's womb safely. Neither Mommy nor Sarah would
have been safe if the doctor had tried to let Sarah be born
through Mommy's vagina. It hurt a bit, but we were so glad
that Sarah was out safely and that Mommy was okay."

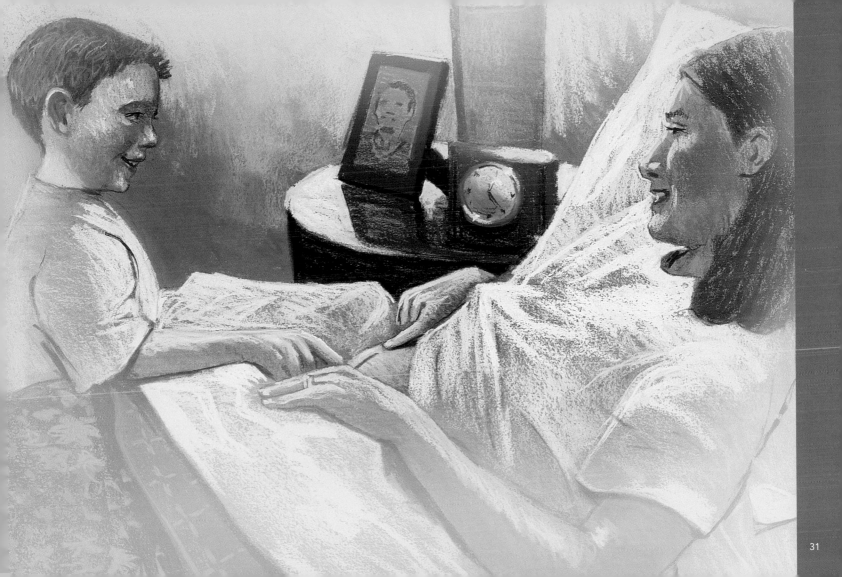

"And when she came out and didn't have the cord to feed her, you fed her from your breasts!"

"God made women's bodies in a wonderful way. Mothers' bodies take the food we eat and make part of it into milk that comes out of our breasts. Our milk is the perfect food for a young baby!"

"What was I like as a baby?"

"You had the most perfect little arms, feet, eyes, and nose. And you had brown eyes and dark, dark hair. The doctor saw right away you had a penis, and that's how she knew you were a boy! You were beautiful. We loved you before you were born, and we loved you even more when we got to hold you."

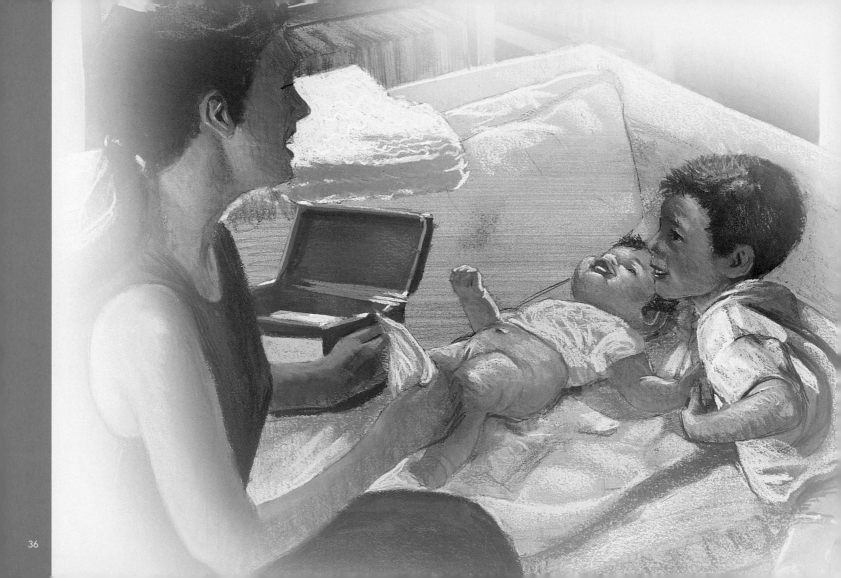

"I have a penis. That makes me a boy like Daddy. I'm glad I'm a boy!"

"I am, too, and so is God! He made you special."

"Girls are special too. God gave Sarah a vagina and a womb, like Mommy, and he didn't give that to you. That makes her a girl. Only girls can become mommies, and only boys can become daddies. God thinks both boys *and* girls are special!"

"But why, Mommy?
Why did God make boys and girls?"

"God made all people to love him and make him happy by obeying his rules. The Bible tells the story of how God made the world. After he made the earth, stars, oceans, plants, and animals, God said that all he had made was 'good.' But on the day God made the first man and the first woman, God said they were 'very good'!"

"Paul, why do you think God said the man and woman were 'very good'?"

"Because the man and woman made God really happy?"

"Yes. They made God very happy because they loved him and loved each other. The Bible says that God is love. Every family full of love is like a good picture of God's love."

"A little boy like you can show Daddy and me you love us by obeying us. Daddy and I try to show God our love by obeying God's good rules.

"We can also show we love each other by hugs and kisses, and by taking care of each other."

"So are all hugs and kisses good?"

"No, not all hugs and kisses are good. If you do not want to share a kiss or a hug or a touch with someone, you don't have to. God does not want anyone to take love from you that you don't want to share."

"And God made your body private. Mommy and I still help you bathe, and a doctor might check every part of your body. Except for that, a boy's penis and a girl's vagina are private. If anyone asks or tries to touch that part of you, you should run right away to let us know. The only other person who will one day get to see your private parts will be your wife, but that's a very long time away!"

"And is that when I might become a daddy?"

"Yes, if God blesses you that way.
And we sure hope he will!"

"I love that story!
I love to know how God made me!"

"It is a wonderful story, Paul. It is one of the most wonderful stories there is."

Before I formed you in the womb I knew you,

and before you were born I consecrated you;

I appointed you a prophet to the nations.

JEREMIAH 1:5

NOTES

1. Stanton L. Jones, "How to Teach Sex: Seven Realities Christians in Every Congregation Need to Know," *Christianity Today* 55, no. 1 (January 2011): 34–39.